ANCIENT EGYPT
INSIDE OUT

Ellen Rodger

 Crabtree Publishing Company

wwww.crabtreebooks.com

Author: Ellen Rodger

Editors: Sarah Eason, Kelly Spence, and Kathy Middleton

Editorial director: Kathy Middleton

Design: Paul Myerscough

Cover design: Paul Myerscough

Photo research: Rachel Blount

Proofreader: Wendy Scavuzzo

**Production coordinator and
 Prepress technician:** Tammy McGarr

Print coordinator: Margaret Amy Salter

Consultant: John Malam, archaeologist

Written and produced for Crabtree Publishing Company
by Calcium Creative

Front Cover
BKGD: Entrance to the Luxor Temple in Egypt built during
the reign of the pharaoh Amenhotep III.
Inset: Two Egyptian rings made from gold, glass, lapis
lazuli, and carnelian inlay.
Title Page
BKGD: The Pyramids of Giza along the Nile, the oldest of
the Seven Wonders of the Ancient World.
Inset: A statue of Hatshepsut, a female pharaoh who began
her reign in 1478 BCE.

Photo Credits:

t=Top, bl=Bottom Left, br=Bottom Right

Alamy: Granger Historical Picture Archive: p. 15tr; Richard
Graulich/The Palm Beach Post/ZUMA Wire: p. 16–17;

LACMA www.lacma.org: The Phil Berg Collection: p. 21b; Gift
of Frank J. and Victoria K. Fertitta: p. 13b;

Shutterstock: Leonid Andronov: p. 10–11; Antpkr: p. 28–29;
Anton_Ivanov: p. 20–21; Everett – Art: p. 6–7, p. 24b; Hallam
creations: p. 8–9; Kokhanchikov: pp. 3, 12–13; Pius Lee: p. 26–27;
Stephen Marques: p. 5l; Pecold: p. 4–5; Serge Vero: p. 1fg, p. 11b;
Hans Wagemaker: p. 14–15; WitR: p. 1bg, p. 19t; The Walters Art
Museum, acquired by Henry Walters: p. 9t, p. 23t;

Wikimedia Commons: Σταύρος: p. 24–25; Carsten Frenzl from
Obernburg, Derutschland: p. 27t; Hermitage Museum: p. 19t.

Map p. 5 by Geoff Ward. Artworks p. 28–29 by Venetia Dean.

Cover: Shutterstock: Alberto Loyo (bg); The Walters Art
Museum, acquired by Henry Walters, 1929 (br).

Library and Archives Canada Cataloguing in Publication

Rodger, Ellen, author
        Ancient Egypt inside out / Ellen Rodger.

(Ancient worlds inside out)
Includes index.
Issued in print and electronic formats.
ISBN 978-0-7787-2874-0 (hardcover).--
ISBN 978-0-7787-2888-7 (softcover).--
ISBN 978-1-4271-1846-2 (HTML)

        1. Egypt--Social life and customs--To 332 B.C.--Juvenile
literature. 2. Egypt--Civilization--To 332 B.C.--Juvenile
literature. 3. Egypt--Antiquities--Juvenile literature. 4. Material
culture--Egypt--Juvenile literature. 5. Egypt--History--To 332
B.C.--Juvenile literature. I. Title.

DT61 R62 2017   j932   C2016-907257-6
                                             C2016-907258-4

Library of Congress Cataloging-in-Publication Data

Names: Rodger, Ellen, author.
Title: Ancient Egypt inside out / Ellen Rodger.
Description: New York, New York : Crabtree Publishing Company,
 [2017] | Series: Ancient Worlds Inside Out | Includes index.
Identifiers: LCCN 2016058589 (print) | LCCN 2016059919 (ebook)
 ISBN 9780778728740 (reinforced library binding : alk. paper) |
 ISBN 9780778728887 (paperback : alkaline paper) |
 ISBN 9781427118462 (Electronic HTML)
Subjects: LCSH: Egypt--Civilization--To 332 B.C.--Juvenile
 literature. | Egypt--Antiquities--Juvenile literature.
Classification: LCC DT61 .R5367 2017 (print) | LCC DT61 (ebook)
 | DDC 932--dc23
LC record available at https://lccn.loc.gov/2016058589

Crabtree Publishing Company

www.crabtreebooks.com   1-800-387-7650

Printed in Canada/032017/EF20170202

Published in Canada
Crabtree Publishing
616 Welland Ave.
St. Catharines, Ontario
L2M 5V6

Published in the United States
Crabtree Publishing
PMB 59051
350 Fifth Avenue, 59th Floor
New York, New York 10118

Published in the United Kingdom
Crabtree Publishing
Maritime House
Basin Road North, Hove
BN41 1WR

Published in Australia
Crabtree Publishing
3 Charles Street
Coburg North
VIC, 3058

CONTENTS

Who Were the Ancient Egyptians?   4

Digging Up the Past   6

The Mighty Nile   8

Pharaohs and Dynasties   10

Daily Life in Ancient Egypt   12

Food, Feasts, and Famine   14

Science and Medicine   16

Technology and Buildings   18

Reading and Writing   20

Gods and the Afterlife   22

Trade and War   24

Enduring Egypt   26

Make Your Own Papyrus Scroll   28

Glossary   30

Learning More   31

Index   32

About the Author   32

WHO WERE THE ANCIENT EGYPTIANS?

The **fertile** lands of the Nile River in northeastern Africa were home to one of the most powerful **civilizations** in the ancient world. Egypt was not the very first ancient civilization, but its well-preserved **remains**—architecture, art, and **artifacts**—are familiar to us. Even thousands of years after its fall, images of pyramids, mummies, tomb art, and **papyrus** scrolls come to mind when we imagine ancient Egypt.

What Is an Ancient Civilization?

Large settlements of people formed the basis of the first civilizations. Through farming, these settlements grew into larger cities. Writing, government, and class systems soon developed. These early settlements led to the later development of present-day cities, states, and countries.

River Civilization

Like many ancient cultures, Egypt was built along the banks of a river. The Nile River is the longest waterway in the world, and runs about 4,132 miles (6,650 km) from its source in Central Africa before emptying into the Mediterranean Sea. Surrounded by desert and green **savannah**, ancient Egyptians depended on the river's life-giving waters and annual floods. The floods enriched the soil with **silt** from the river. The silt **fertilized** crops and made it possible for an agricultural civilization to thrive on its banks.

From Scattered Villages to a Kingdom

Egypt did more than survive on the banks of the Nile—it flourished. A ready and available food supply allowed the population to grow. Villages grew up along the river, eventually forming into distinct regions known as the "two lands," or Upper and Lower Egypt. Ancient Egyptians developed sophisticated systems of government in which kings, and occasionally queens, called pharaohs ruled the land. A large workforce built cities and monuments, and a strong army protected the Egyptians from outside **invaders**. Around 3100 B.C.E., the two lands united into one powerful kingdom.

Once home to crocodiles and hippopotamuses, the Nile River was a major transportation route. The ancient Egyptians built sailboats and **barges** to travel from city to city and beyond.

Key

Ancient Egypt around the year 330 B.C.E.

Present-day borders

Israel

Mediterranean Sea

Rosetta

Alexandria

Jordan

Giza ● Cairo

Egypt

Egypt

This map shows Egypt and the Nile River delta, which is located on the coast of the Mediterranean Sea. A delta is at a river's mouth, where it diverts into many branches.

Nile River

EASTERN DESERT

Saudi Arabia

Red Sea

Luxor

WESTERN DESERT

Libya

Abu Simbel ●

Sudan

DIGGING UP THE PAST

"FOUND! Entrance to the Amun Ra Pyramid! Discovery of the Century!" Around the world, newspaper headlines announced the discovery of King Tutankhamun's tomb in 1922. After almost a decade of searching, British **Egyptologist** Howard Carter had located the burial place of King Tut, which had lain untouched for more than 3,400 years. The discovery kicked off a craze for all things Egyptian, and launched a new era of archaeological discovery.

Digging Up the Past

Hundreds of years ago, people used ancient writings, folk history, geographic maps, and information passed on by local residents to determine where ancient peoples might have lived. Today, **archaeologists** examine sites of interest to determine their history. They use tools such as **aerial photography** or **drone** cameras to figure out where to dig. When they excavate, or dig, they are careful to do it in a way that will not damage any artifacts or remains they might find.

History in an Object

The objects that archaeologists find can reveal a lot about an ancient culture. A piece of ancient paper made from papyrus, for example, shows that the Egyptians had the knowledge, the tools, and the need to make paper. Papyrus is a reed that grows on the banks of the Nile. Its stalk was pounded and pressed into paper. The thick paper was used for writing on, for everything from medical and math scrolls to histories of kings and pharaohs. From these and other papyrus scrolls, we have learned that the ancient Egyptians developed systems of writing to record their knowledge.

King Tut's tomb was decorated with art. His sarcophagus, or funeral container, held the body of the 18-year-old king. It was found in a coffin contained inside two other coffins.

What Are Primary Sources?

Archaeology is the study of how people lived in the past. Archaeologists learn about how and where people lived through the materials they left behind. These raw materials, called **primary sources**, were made during a specific period of time. Primary sources include artifacts, such as pottery or tools, and written documents such as records of death. Examining primary sources gives us clues about how people lived long ago, and how great civilizations flourished. Archaeologists **analyze**, or examine, these objects to **interpret**, or figure out, their meanings.

THE MIGHTY NILE

The ancient Egyptians called the land on the banks of the Nile *kemet*, meaning "black land." This refers to the rich dark soil that surrounds the Nile River. Without the Nile, Egyptian civilization would not exist. In fact, around 450 B.C.E., the ancient Greek historian Herodotus wrote that "Egypt was the gift of the Nile" because the civilization owed its existence and very survival to the river.

River and Desert

The Nile River is Egypt's major source of fresh water. In the ancient Egyptian language, it was simply called *Iteru*, or river. People lived there long before the Egyptians, and as early as the **Neolithic period**, which began around 10,000 B.C.E. Most of the population of ancient Egypt lived along its banks in farm villages or major cities. The lands the Egyptians called "red land," or desert, surrounded the Nile on both sides. The red sands of the Eastern Desert bordered the river and the Red Sea. The Western Desert was home to several **oases**, or areas with water from underground rivers and springs, where date palms, vegetables, and other plants grew. These oases were important stops for travelers and traders.

Upper and Lower Egypt

Egypt was divided into Upper and Lower Egypt. Upper Egypt was in the south, and included a narrow valley with high cliffs and the cities of Memphis and Abu. Below Upper Egypt were the kingdoms of Nubia and Kush (present-day southern Egypt and Sudan). Lower Egypt was in the north and included the delta, marshlands, and mouth of the Nile, ending at the Red Sea.

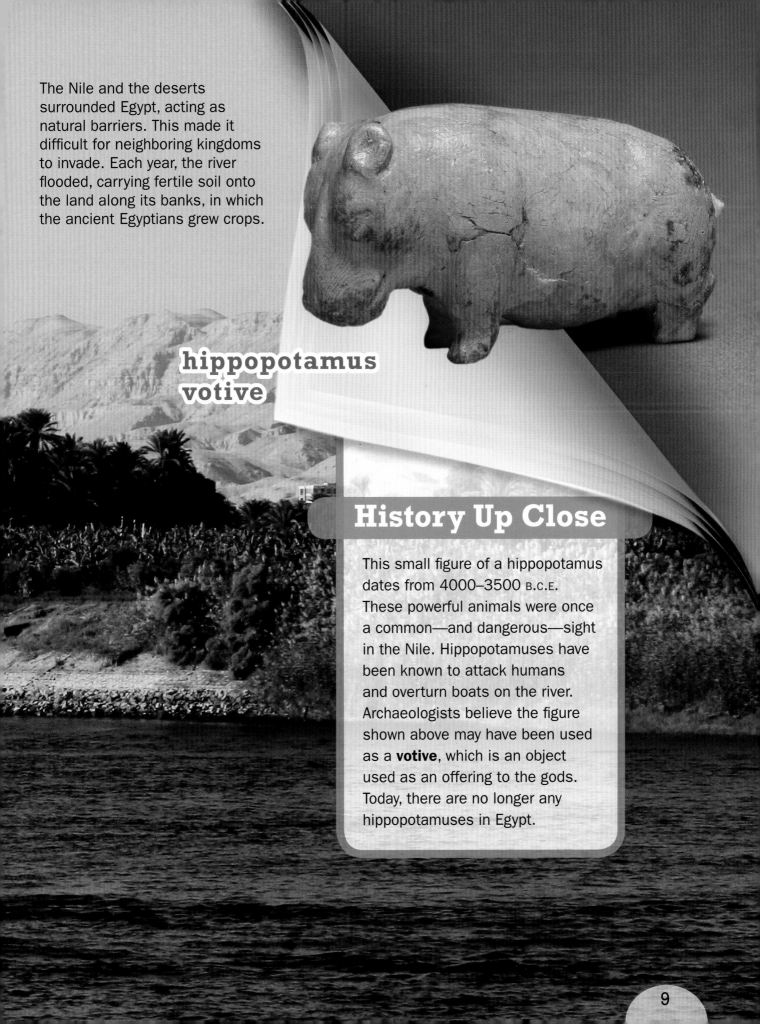

The Nile and the deserts surrounded Egypt, acting as natural barriers. This made it difficult for neighboring kingdoms to invade. Each year, the river flooded, carrying fertile soil onto the land along its banks, in which the ancient Egyptians grew crops.

hippopotamus votive

History Up Close

This small figure of a hippopotamus dates from 4000–3500 B.C.E. These powerful animals were once a common—and dangerous—sight in the Nile. Hippopotamuses have been known to attack humans and overturn boats on the river. Archaeologists believe the figure shown above may have been used as a **votive**, which is an object used as an offering to the gods. Today, there are no longer any hippopotamuses in Egypt.

PHARAOHS AND DYNASTIES

Ancient Egypt, as we call it today, was a civilization that is believed to have lasted about 3,000 years. During that period, many kings called pharaohs ruled the land from 30 different **dynasties**. Historians and archaeologists group ancient Egyptian history into periods and kingdoms to easily keep track of the changes in culture and government, as well as the advances made by each.

Dynasties and Pharaohs

A dynasty is a line of rulers **descended** from one person or family. The first Egyptian dynasty began around 3100 B.C.E. with the pharaoh Narmer. There were kings before Narmer, but he is credited with uniting the two kingdoms of Upper and Lower Egypt. Narmer set up a capital city at Memphis, which has been known by many names over its long history. Over thousands of years, the power and wealth of the pharaohs increased. Pharaohs ruled over the people. They were considered the high priests of every temple and were believed to be gods on Earth. Pharaohs owned all the land, made laws, and declared war on other peoples.

Ruling the Kingdom

Pharaohs needed trusted advisers to carry out orders, and a tremendous number of workers so they could build monuments to their reign. The **vizier** was the chief government administrator appointed by the pharaoh to carry out orders. Taxes were collected by the pharaoh's treasurer in the form of grain, property, and goods. These taxes added to the pharaoh's wealth and also supported the army. Soldiers were usually peasant farmers forced into the army to protect Egypt from invaders. Writers, called scribes, were educated members of mostly noble families. They wrote official documents.

Dig Deeper!

How would we know Hatshepsut was a pharaoh from looking at her images?

The Karnak Temple in Luxor once included images of the female pharaoh Hatshepsut. It was uncommon for a female to become pharaoh, and Thutmose III ordered the destruction of her images when he became pharaoh.

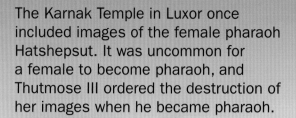

History Up Close

This statue of Hatshepsut is part of the temple at Deir el-Bahri. She was the wife of pharaoh Thutmose II, who was also her half brother. To keep power within the family, pharaohs often married their close relatives, but also had many other wives. After Thutmose II died, Hatshepsut crowned herself pharaoh, ruling on behalf of her stepson Thutmose III. She was known as a good ruler who ordered the construction of many temples and trade routes. On temple art, Hatshepsut is shown holding the crook and flail—tools used by shepherds—and a false beard. All of these things were symbols of royalty.

Hatshepsut statue

DAILY LIFE IN ANCIENT EGYPT

Most of the surviving artifacts of ancient Egypt give only small clues as to how ordinary Egyptians lived. Historians and archaeologists use many different primary sources to piece together the everyday history of ancient Egypt. These sources include tomb art and inscriptions, papyrus scrolls, materials found at archaeological sites, and accounts written by foreign travelers.

Farmers, Workers, and Slaves

Ancient records reveal that about 80 percent of Egyptians were farmers, workers, and slaves. They lived in houses made from mud bricks and stone. Children lived and worked alongside their parents and were cared for by their mothers. We know children played with toys and games because it is pictured in the art on the walls of some tombs. Instead of using money, people **bartered** and traded items or work. **Excavations** show that workers lived, died, and were buried in villages built near the pyramids they worked on. Farmers were also recruited to build pyramids during the flood season. Farmers lived in homes with dirt floors in small villages near the fields along the banks of the Nile. Like pyramid workers, skilled craftspeople such as rock cutters and sculptors worked for the pharaoh. Slaves, who were often **prisoners of war** or criminals, worked as servants for wealthy families and nobles.

Pharaohs and the Nobles

Pharaohs and their families, as well as the vizier, nobles, and priests were wealthy. They were at the top of the social **hierarchy** in ancient Egypt. Pharaohs lived in palaces and displayed their wealth by wearing fine jewelry. Nobles held government jobs, and often owned farm land or became wealthy from tax collection.

Tomb art has revealed a lot about everyday life in ancient Egypt, including clothing, rituals, and religion.

History Up Close

From the pharaoh to a farmer, all ancient Egyptians wore makeup. The container shown below dates from 1410–1372 B.C.E. It belonged to Queen Tiye, the wife of Amenhotep III. The container was used to store kohl, an eyeliner made from ground metals mixed with fats and oils. A long stick was used to combine the ingredients together inside the tubes. The tip of the stick was then used to apply the makeup around a person's eyes. Green and black were popular colors.

kohl container

FOODS, FEASTS, AND FAMINE

Farming allowed Egypt to grow from a collection of villages on the Nile River to a thriving civilization that flourished for thousands of years. The ancient Egyptians developed a system of agriculture and a yearly calendar based on the Nile River's cycle of flooding. The river and its effect on farming were so important that ancient Egyptians made sacrifices and worshiped gods of the flood or river.

What Did They Grow and Eat?

The silt deposited in the floodplain of the Nile River enriched the soil near its banks. Farmers plowed and seeded the land. Over time, they also developed **irrigation** systems to water crops. They grew a number of crops to eat, including wheat, barley, onions, cabbages, lettuce, lentils, and beans, as well as flax for making linen clothing. Ancient Egyptians also grew fruit such as dates and figs. They raised animals for meat, and also hunted and fished. Archaeologists digging at a site near the pyramids at Giza found that pyramid workers ate a diet rich in sheep, goat, cattle, and pig meat, as well as bread and beer. The workers needed hearty foods because they used up so many **calories** building the pyramids.

Marking the Seasons

Farmers in Egypt divided the year into three seasons based on flooding, growing, and harvesting. The flooding season, or Akhet, lasted from June until September. There was little farm work to do when the fields were flooded, so farmers were recruited to build pyramids and temples. The growing season, or Peret, followed from October to February. Shemu, the harvest season, took place from March to May. Sometimes the Nile did not flood. If the pharaoh did not have enough grain stored, it could result in **famine** and starvation for much of the population.

farming tomb art

History Up Close

Art from ancient Egyptian tombs often featured images of everyday life. This painting dates from 1450 B.C.E. Farmers are shown sowing and harvesting wheat. Curved tools called **sickles** were used to cut the stalks of wheat, which were then carried away in baskets to be **threshed**. Tomb paintings such as this one were meant to ensure that the deceased person would continue to receive food or nourishment in the **afterlife** and that their family would prosper.

Today, Egyptians still farm the fertile soils along the banks of the Nile.

SCIENCE AND MEDICINE

The ancient Egyptians were knowledgeable scientists and **innovators**. Their knowledge of medicine and anatomy was known throughout the ancient world. Some Egyptian innovations, such as toothpaste, perfume cones, or simple medicines, made everyday life easier or more enjoyable. Other innovations, such as the complex process for making mummies, proved the ancient Egyptians had an understanding of anatomy.

Vain Inspiration

Many Egyptian paintings show well-dressed men and women in wigs and makeup. They were obsessed with beauty, and made razors, wigs, perfume, and toothpaste to improve their appearance. Egyptian toothpaste was made from burned eggshells, ash, or powdered animal hooves. The **abrasive**, or rough, material was combined with honey to clean teeth. Ancient Egyptians used razors to shave their heads, faces, and bodies, then wore wigs made from real hair. Both women and men used makeup and wore perfumed cones of fat on their heads that melted and left them smelling sweet.

Medical Knowledge

Doctors in ancient Egypt could set broken bones, treat illnesses with odd concoctions, and even perform minor surgery. They used sophisticated surgical tools such as hooks, **pincers**, drills, and **forceps**. These tools were handy for mummifying, or preparing bodies after death. The eight-step mummification process took up to 70 days and required the removal of organs. The bodies were then dried with a chemical, stuffed with linen, and wrapped.

Mummies were prepared for the afterlife, where it was believed the dead person would return to their body and live on.

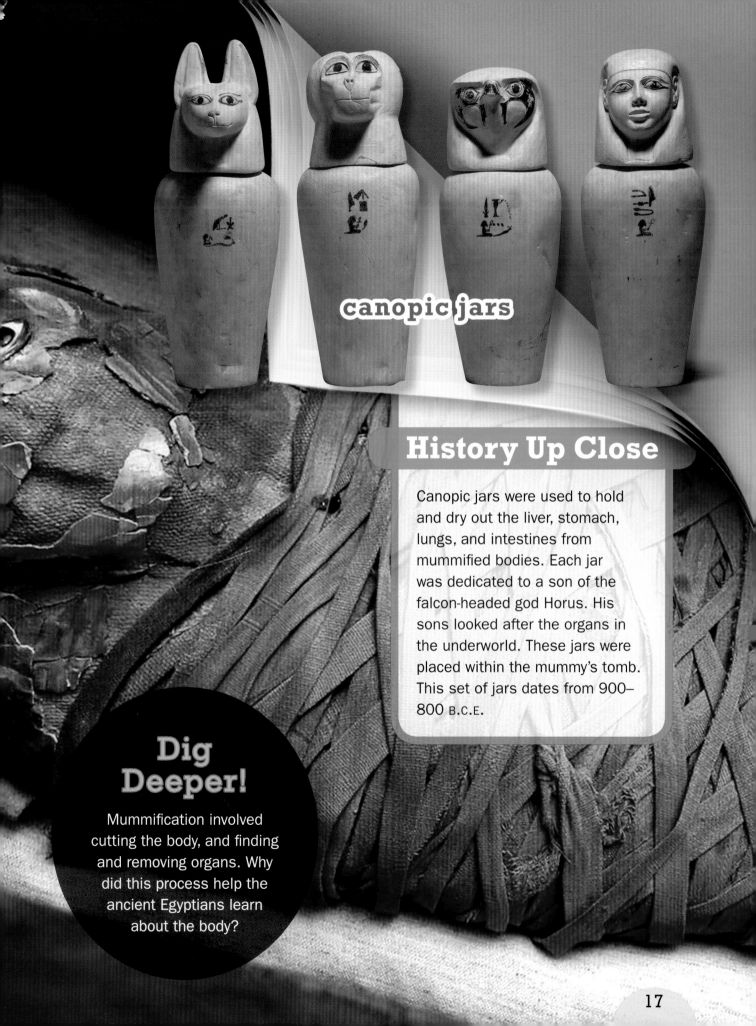

canopic jars

History Up Close

Canopic jars were used to hold and dry out the liver, stomach, lungs, and intestines from mummified bodies. Each jar was dedicated to a son of the falcon-headed god Horus. His sons looked after the organs in the underworld. These jars were placed within the mummy's tomb. This set of jars dates from 900–800 B.C.E.

Dig Deeper!

Mummification involved cutting the body, and finding and removing organs. Why did this process help the ancient Egyptians learn about the body?

TECHNOLOGY AND BUILDINGS

Ask people what comes to mind when you mention ancient Egypt. Most likely it will be the pyramids. The memory of ancient Egypt survives in part because of its magnificent and sturdy buildings. They built pyramids, tombs, and other structures that have lasted thousands of years.

The Great Pyramid of Giza (right) stands 453 feet (138 m) tall. About 2.3 million blocks were needed to build this majestic tomb.

Ancient Technology

The ancient Egyptians invented simple machines and developed methods of building and making things that have stood the test of time. One simple machine still in use is the shaduf—a device that made drawing water from the Nile easier for farmers. The shaduf is a bucket hanging from a rope on the end of a pole with a heavy weight on the other end. It lifts heavy containers of water from the river to be dumped into canals used for irrigation.

Pyramid Technology

There were no digging machines or heavy equipment in ancient Egypt. Pyramids and temples were built by hand by a workforce of thousands of men. Construction techniques changed over time, but the pyramids were usually built from quarried limestone. The Great Pyramid of Giza is 4,500 years old, and is the largest stone structure in the world. It was built as a tomb for King Khufu. The blocks of stone used in construction were raised on zigzagging ramps. But even after hundreds of years of research, historians still debate exactly how the pyramids were built.

History Up Close

A pyramidion was the last stone lifted into place on top of a pyramid. It was made of different materials, such as granite and limestone. This limestone pyramidion from the 7th century B.C.E. was discovered in Abydos, where it topped the tomb of a priest named Rer. Also known as a *benbenet*, some archaeologists believe these stones represented a connection between the dead person and the Sun god Ra. Thousands of years ago, this pyramidion might have been coated in gold so it would shine in the Sun.

pyramidion

READING AND WRITING

Imagine writing using 700 pictures instead of 26 letters. The writing seen on ancient Egyptian temple walls and papyrus scrolls is one of the oldest writing systems in the world. It dates back to between 3400 and 3200 B.C.E.

Three Forms

The ancient Egyptian language was written in three forms: hieroglyphic, hieratic, and demotic. They were developed and used at different times in history, but each form used a combination of symbols and **pictographs**, or symbols used for a word or phrase. Hieroglyphs were used for inscriptions on temples and monuments. Hieratic script was used for government documents. They were used from 3200 B.C.E. until 400 C.E. Demotic writing developed later than hieroglyphic script.

Lost Writing

For thousands of years, Egyptians used hieroglyphs, hieratic, or demotic script on art and official documents. By 400 C.E., these forms of writing were no longer used. Eventually, the ability to read and write ancient Egyptian scripts was lost. However, in 1799, a French soldier found a black stone carved with hieroglyphs, demotic script, and ancient Greek in the Nile Delta town of Rosetta. The three scripts contained the same message. Since historians knew how to read ancient Greek, the Rosetta Stone became the key to **deciphering**, or decoding, the lost Egyptian language.

Books and Knowledge

The Book of the Dead sounds like the title of a horror story, but it is more like a guide to the ancient Egyptian afterlife. Written on a number of papyrus scrolls, it listed magic spells and religious chants that assisted a dead person on their journey to the underworld. The scrolls are written in hieroglyphic and hieratic script.

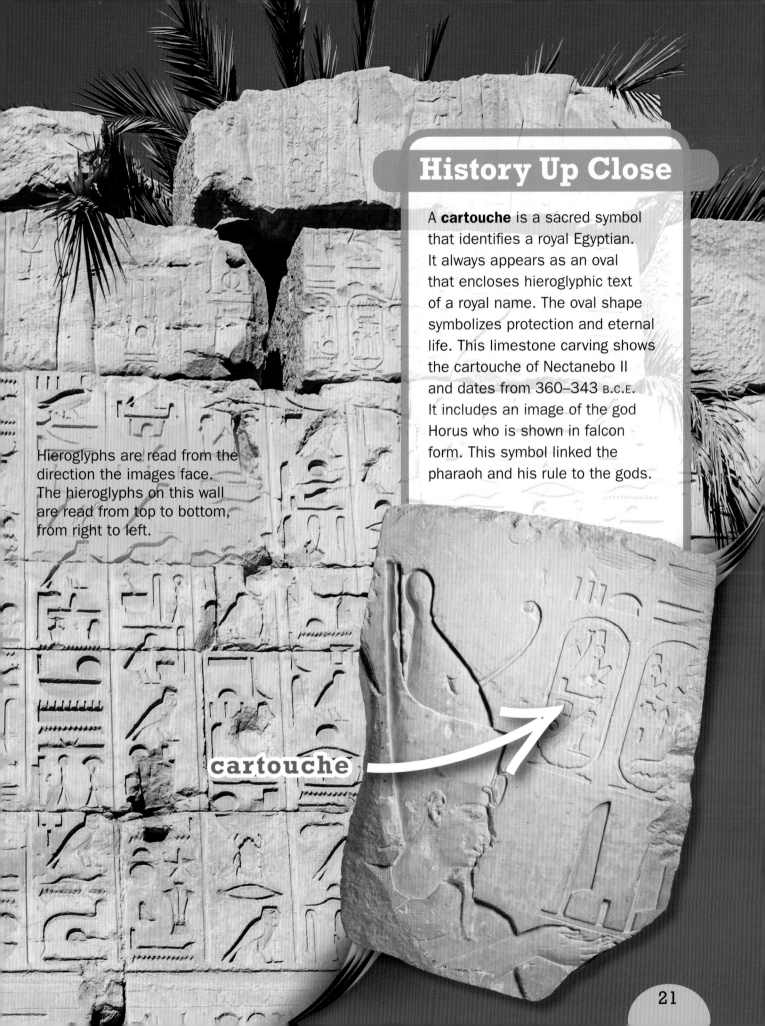

History Up Close

A **cartouche** is a sacred symbol that identifies a royal Egyptian. It always appears as an oval that encloses hieroglyphic text of a royal name. The oval shape symbolizes protection and eternal life. This limestone carving shows the cartouche of Nectanebo II and dates from 360–343 B.C.E. It includes an image of the god Horus who is shown in falcon form. This symbol linked the pharaoh and his rule to the gods.

Hieroglyphs are read from the direction the images face. The hieroglyphs on this wall are read from top to bottom, from right to left.

cartouche

GODS AND THE AFTERLIFE

The ancient Egyptians didn't take any chances. They had a god or goddess for almost every situation or place—an estimated 2,000 of them in total. Some were local gods, who protected farmers. Other gods, such as the Sun god Ra or Re; Osiris, the god of the underworld; or mother goddess Isis, were more powerful or widely worshiped. Ancient Egyptians honored different gods at different times in history.

Godly Adoration

Temples were places where gods were worshiped, rituals were performed, and festivals were held. Temples were believed to be the homes of gods and goddesses and were filled with their statues. Although each temple was dedicated to one god, other gods could also be worshiped there. The pharaoh was the chief priest, judge, and lawmaker. As a god on Earth, he was also a direct link to the other gods. The pharaoh kept *Ma'at*, or order, balance, and justice, in the world by maintaining a good relationship with the gods.

The Afterlife

In the ancient Egyptian belief system, death marked the end of one journey and the start of another. The evidence from pyramids and tombs shows they were strict about death rituals. After death, a person's spirit was said to leave the body temporarily, then return to it in the afterlife. This is why Egyptians mummified dead bodies—they believed that a person could only live in the afterlife with a body. The bodies of pharaohs and wealthy people were placed in elaborate tombs filled with food and goods they might need, such as chariots, games, or art.

Anubis, the god of the dead, mummies, and magic, is often shown with the head of a jackal.

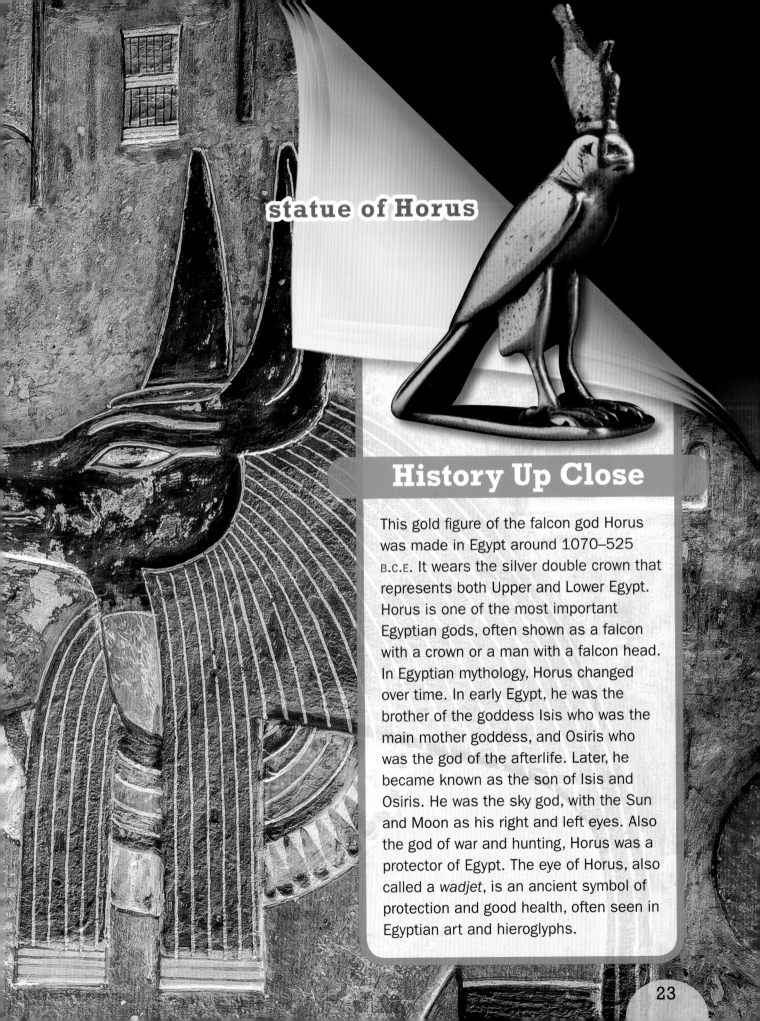

statue of Horus

History Up Close

This gold figure of the falcon god Horus was made in Egypt around 1070–525 B.C.E. It wears the silver double crown that represents both Upper and Lower Egypt. Horus is one of the most important Egyptian gods, often shown as a falcon with a crown or a man with a falcon head. In Egyptian mythology, Horus changed over time. In early Egypt, he was the brother of the goddess Isis who was the main mother goddess, and Osiris who was the god of the afterlife. Later, he became known as the son of Isis and Osiris. He was the sky god, with the Sun and Moon as his right and left eyes. Also the god of war and hunting, Horus was a protector of Egypt. The eye of Horus, also called a *wadjet*, is an ancient symbol of protection and good health, often seen in Egyptian art and hieroglyphs.

TRADE AND WAR

Civilizations come and go. Some begin and reach their peak in less than 500 years. Ancient Egypt was a long-lasting civilization, with historians dividing it up into several time periods lasting 3,000 years in total. During that long history, ancient Egypt was at times isolated. At other times, it had thriving relationships with other great civilizations.

Trade and Trading Partners

Egypt was a land rich in certain resources. Along the Nile, rich farmland allowed people to grow large amounts of food and grow flax, which was made into linen. In the deserts, there were deposits of gold and other **minerals**. But there were things that Egyptians desired that could not be found within their own borders. To get these things, the ancient Egyptians traveled by boat along the Nile, and across the sea, as well as over the deserts to trade with other major civilizations, such as Mesopotamia to the east. They got wood to build ships from the northeastern area that is now Lebanon. Beautiful stones for decoration such as **obsidian** came from Ethiopia to the south, and lapis lazuli from Afghanistan to the east. Incense, spices, myrrh, and precious oils used for religious rituals came from Punt, a region to the south of Egypt. In return, the Egyptians traded gold, papyrus, linen, and grain.

Wars and Decline

For many years, the harsh environment of the deserts and Egypt's vast army protected ancient Egyptians from most invaders. But Egypt was challenged at different times by the Libyans from the west, Nubians or Kushites from the south, and Canaanites from the north. The Hyksos, a people from the east, gained control of the city of Memphis in 1700 B.C.E. before being driven out of Egypt. Later, the Assyrians and Persians invaded and took over parts of Egypt. By 332 B.C.E., the Macedonian king Alexander the Great had conquered Egypt, founding the city of Alexandria on the Mediterranean Sea. After his death, his general Ptolemy I made himself pharaoh of Egypt. His descendants adopted Egyptian culture and ruled for another 300 years. The last ruler was Cleopatra, who remained in power until Egypt became part of the Roman Empire in 30 B.C.E.

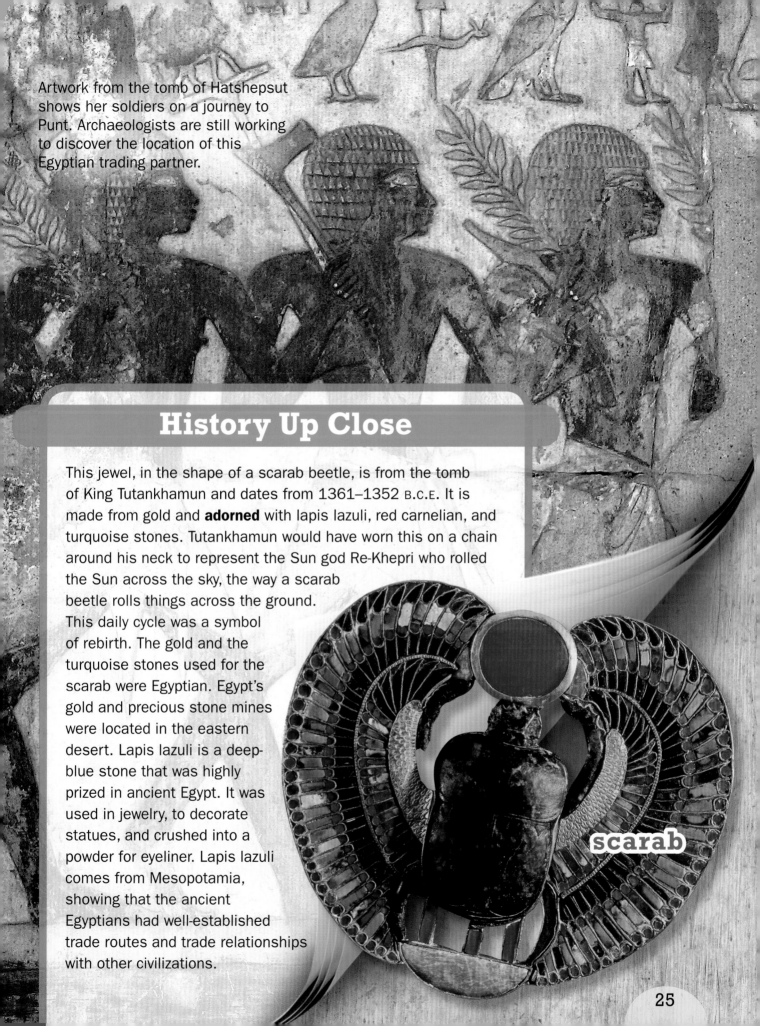

Artwork from the tomb of Hatshepsut shows her soldiers on a journey to Punt. Archaeologists are still working to discover the location of this Egyptian trading partner.

History Up Close

This jewel, in the shape of a scarab beetle, is from the tomb of King Tutankhamun and dates from 1361–1352 B.C.E. It is made from gold and **adorned** with lapis lazuli, red carnelian, and turquoise stones. Tutankhamun would have worn this on a chain around his neck to represent the Sun god Re-Khepri who rolled the Sun across the sky, the way a scarab beetle rolls things across the ground. This daily cycle was a symbol of rebirth. The gold and the turquoise stones used for the scarab were Egyptian. Egypt's gold and precious stone mines were located in the eastern desert. Lapis lazuli is a deep-blue stone that was highly prized in ancient Egypt. It was used in jewelry, to decorate statues, and crushed into a powder for eyeliner. Lapis lazuli comes from Mesopotamia, showing that the ancient Egyptians had well-established trade routes and trade relationships with other civilizations.

scarab

25

ENDURING EGYPT

Ancient Egyptian history and culture fascinated later civilizations. Even conquerors of Egypt, such as the Romans, were in awe of the pyramids and monuments, borrowing Egyptian design and style for their own buildings. Ancient Egypt still fascinates people today, and archaeologists continue to make new discoveries that add to the knowledge of this captivating civilization. The study of ancient Egypt even has its own name: Egyptology.

Studying Ancient Egypt

In 1954, a ship was discovered sealed in a pit at the Great Pyramid of Giza. It was built for the pharaoh Khufu. Some people believe the vessel was used to carry the pharaoh's body along the Nile to his majestic tomb. The ship was reconstructed over many years by an archaeologist who first studied the images in carvings of ships and wooden models of ships from tombs. He also studied modern Egyptian boatbuilding to compare the two methods. Archaeologists and **anthropologists** examine the physical evidence of a culture through its objects and architecture. This evidence is called material culture. Archaeologists are like puzzle solvers who search for use or meaning in the object. But sometimes the true meaning does not present itself until much later.

Egyptomania

Interest in ancient Egypt is not new, but European exploration of Egypt in the late 1700s led to a craze for all things Egyptian. This interest, called Egyptomania, led to increased excavations of pyramids, resulting in the discovery of the tomb of King Tutankhamun in 1922. The world was fascinated to read stories about "King Tut." A legend about the mummy's curse said that anyone who disturbed a buried mummy would be doomed to suffer bad luck or death. Some of Tut's discoverers did die soon after. Tutankhamun's tomb was one of the greatest archaeological discoveries of the 1900s. The tomb had been buried in sand for centuries, keeping it safe from tomb robbers. The finely crafted objects, gold mask, coffin, and chariots remained untouched. The riches of Tut's tomb have toured the world through museum exhibits, making this young king one of the most famous pharaohs of all.

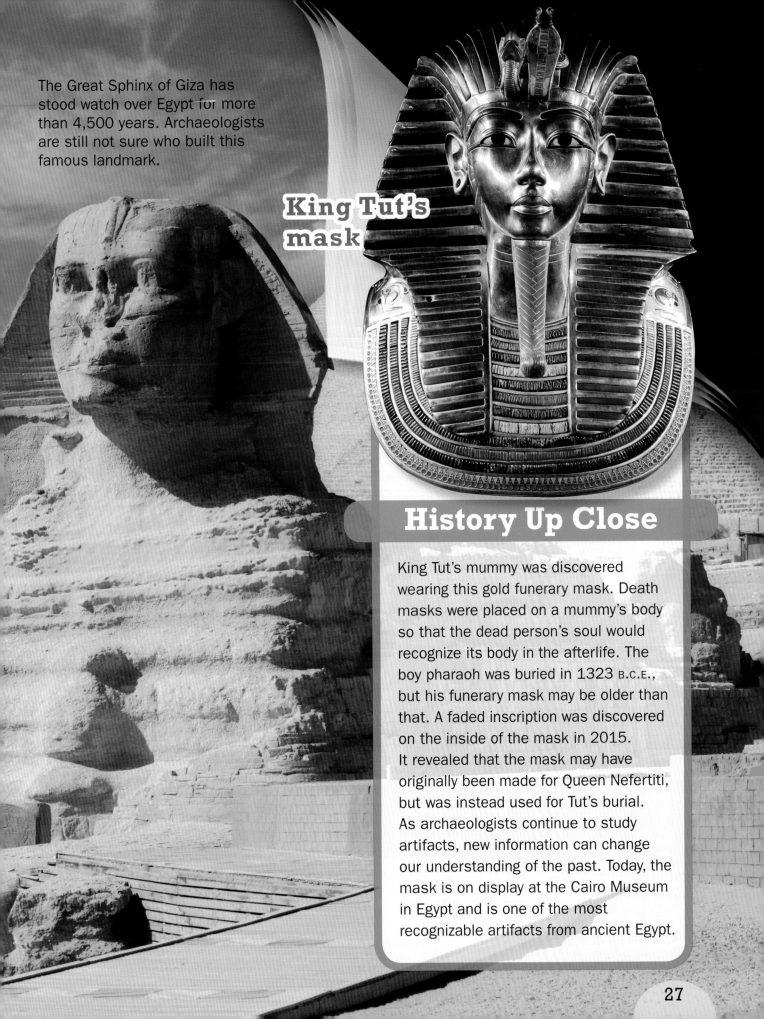

The Great Sphinx of Giza has stood watch over Egypt for more than 4,500 years. Archaeologists are still not sure who built this famous landmark.

King Tut's mask

History Up Close

King Tut's mummy was discovered wearing this gold funerary mask. Death masks were placed on a mummy's body so that the dead person's soul would recognize its body in the afterlife. The boy pharaoh was buried in 1323 B.C.E., but his funerary mask may be older than that. A faded inscription was discovered on the inside of the mask in 2015. It revealed that the mask may have originally been made for Queen Nefertiti, but was instead used for Tut's burial. As archaeologists continue to study artifacts, new information can change our understanding of the past. Today, the mask is on display at the Cairo Museum in Egypt and is one of the most recognizable artifacts from ancient Egypt.

MAKE YOUR OWN PAPYRUS SCROLL

Papyrus is a tall plant that grows in the marshes of the Nile River. Ancient Egyptians used it to make reed baskets, ropes, sandals, mats, paper, and even boats. First made around 4000 B.C.E., papyrus paper was thick and strong. Papyrus scrolls were glued together and rolled. Some ancient scrolls were more than 100 feet (30 m) long.

How Was Papyrus Made?

Papyrus was made by cutting stems from the plant, pounding them flat, and soaking them. The strips of papyrus were overlapped, pressed to remove excess moisture, then dried. Archaeologists recreate processes such as this to learn more about ancient cultures.

This is the Egyptian alphabet adapted to match the alphabet we use today. This is called a **transliteration**.

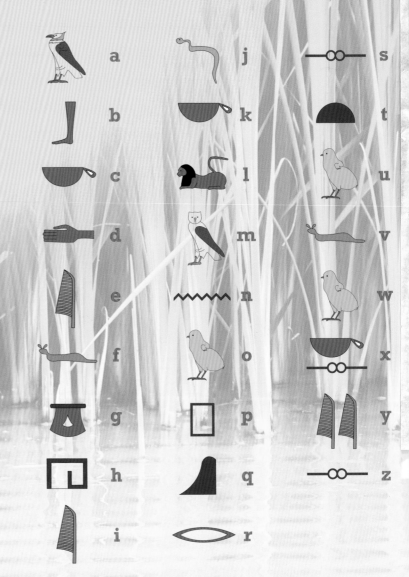

Activity:

Make Papyrus

Write your own message in hieroglyphs!

You Will Need:

- Newspaper
- Paper bag
- Plastic tub
- 1/2 cup (125 ml) of water
- 1/2 cup (125 ml) of white glue
- Paper towels
- Colored pencils

Instructions

1. Cover a workspace, such as a kitchen table, with a layer of newspaper.
2. Tear the paper bag into several long strips.
3. In a plastic tub, mix together 1/2 cup (125 ml) of water and 1/2 cup (125 ml) of white glue.
4. Set a sheet of paper towel on your workspace.
5. Dip the strips of paper into the glue mixture. Use your fingers to remove any excess glue.
6. Lay a layer of strips across the paper towel. Then cover the first layer with a second layer, going cross-wise. Let it dry.
7. Use the alphabet on the opposite page to write a message using Egyptian hieroglyphs with colored pencils.

The Challenge

When the paper is completely dry, you can write on it, roll it like a scroll, or fold it. Use the Egyptian hieroglyphs on the opposite page to write a message on the sheet using colored pencils. Have a friend decode your message, just like a historian.

step 5

step 6

GLOSSARY

Note: Some bold-faced words are defined where they appear in the text.

adorned Made beautiful or attractive

aerial photography Taking photographs of features on the ground from an airplane

afterlife Life after death

anthropologists People who study human societies and cultures, and their development

archaeologists People who study the artifacts left by people who lived in the past

artifacts Objects made by humans that give information about a culture or historical way of life

barges Flat-bottomed boats used to carry freight, usually along waterways

bartered Exchanged items or services rather than paid money to buy something

calories Energy gained from or contained in food

civilizations The societies, cultures, or ways of life of an area

conquerors People that overcome others by force

descended To be a direct blood relative of someone

drone A remote-controlled aircraft that takes pictures

dynasties A series of rulers who all come from the same family

Egyptologist Someone who studies the history and civilization of ancient Egypt

excavations Sites that have been dug out

famine An extreme shortage of food, which often leads to widespread hunger and death

fertile Describing something, such as land or soil, that is capable of producing lots of plants or crops

fertilized Added substances to make soil productive

forceps Tools used to grasp and hold, often during medical procedures

hierarchy A system in which groups of people or things are ranked one above the other according to status

innovators People who introduce new ideas, products, or ways of doing things

inscriptions Words written on a wall, on a piece of art, or in a book

invaders A group that enters a country to take it over

irrigation A process in which water is transported to areas for agriculture

minerals Solid, naturally occurring substances found underground

Neolithic period The later part of the Stone Age, in which tools made of stone were used

obsidian A dark, glass-like volcanic rock

papyrus A plant that grows on the banks of the Nile and also a type of paper made from the plant

pincers Tools that are used to grip

primary sources Materials, such as tools or written documents, created during a specific period of time being studied

prisoners of war People, especially soldiers, who are captured and imprisoned by the enemy during war

remains A person's or animal's body after death, or the parts of something that are left over

savannah A grassy plain with few trees

sickles Farming tools with curved blades used to cut crops, such as wheat

silt Sand or soil that is carried by water and sinks to the bottom

threshed Separated the seeds from the plants with a machine or tool

transliteration To write words or letters in the characters of another alphabet

votive An object, such as a candle, offered in fulfillment of an oath or vow

Learning More

Want to learn more about ancient Egypt? Check out these resources.

Books

Baker Moore, Shannon. *King Tut's Tomb*. ABDO Publishing, 2015.

Boyer, Crispin. *Everything Ancient Egypt*. National Geographic Children's Books, 2012.

Hart, John. *Eyewitness: Ancient Egypt*. Dorling Kindersley, 2014.

Malam, John. *The Egyptians*. PowerKids Press, 2011.

Rubalcaba, Jill. *Ancient Egypt: Archaeology Unlocks the Secrets of Egypt's Past*. National Geographic Children's Books, 2006.

Turner, Tracey. *Hard as Nails in Ancient Egypt*. Crabtree Publishing, 2015.

Websites

Explore ancient Egypt on this interactive site from the British Museum, which includes many artifacts from this fascinating culture.
www.ancientegypt.co.uk

The Canadian Museum of History presents an online exhibition on ancient Egypt.
www.historymuseum.ca/cmc/exhibitions/civil/egypt/egypte.shtml

Take a detailed look at the Great Pyramid of Giza in this comprehensive site from National Geographic.
www.nationalgeographic.com/pyramids/khufu.html

This site hosts an online exhibit on the mummification process.
www.ancientegypt.co.uk/mummies/story/page2.html

Explore the ship uncovered near the Great Pyramid of Giza in this online presentation from PBS.
www.pbs.org/wgbh/nova/pharaoh/expl-nf.html

Smart History presents a comprehensive list of articles and videos on ancient Egypt, along with several examples of artifacts.
https://smarthistory.org/ancient-egypt

INDEX

afterlife 15, 16, 20, 22–23, 27
ancient civilization defined 4
Anubis 22–23
archaeologists 6, 7, 9, 10, 12, 14, 19, 25, 26, 27, 28

bartering 12
beauty 16
Book of the Dead 20

canopic jars 17
Carter, Howard 6
cartouches 21

doctors and medicine 16
dynasties 10

Egyptology 26–27
Egyptomania 26

farming 4, 9, 10, 12, 14–15, 24
foods 14, 15

gods and goddesses 19, 22–23
Great Pyramid of Giza 18–19
Great Sphinx 26–27

Hatshepsut 11, 25
hierarchy 12
hieroglyphs 20–21, 23, 28, 29
hippopotamuses 5, 9
Horus 23

Isis 22, 23

Karnak Temple 11
kohl 13

lapis lazuli 24, 25

makeup 13, 16
making papyrus 28–29
map 5
mummification 16–17, 22, 27

Narmer 10
Nile River 4, 5, 8, 9, 12, 14–15
nobles 10, 12

oases 8
Osiris 22, 23

paper-making 6, 28–29
papyrus 6, 28–29
perfume cones 16

pharaohs 10, 11, 12, 13, 21, 22, 24, 26, 27
primary sources 7
pyramidions 19
pyramids 18–19

Ra 19, 22
Rosetta Stone 20

seasons 14
slaves 12
systems of government 4

taxes 10
Thutmose III 11
tomb art 6–7, 12–13, 15, 22–23, 24–25
tomb exploration 26–27
toothpaste 16
trading goods 24–25
Tutankhamun, King 6, 25, 26, 27

Upper and Lower Egypt 4, 8

viziers 10
votives 9

wars 24
writing 20–21

ABOUT THE AUTHOR

Growing up, Ellen Rodger was fascinated with mummies, including King Tut, mummy horror movies, and the real Egyptian mummy exhibited in her small hometown museum. She has edited books on ancient civilizations, mythology, and explorers, and is the author of many books for children and adults.